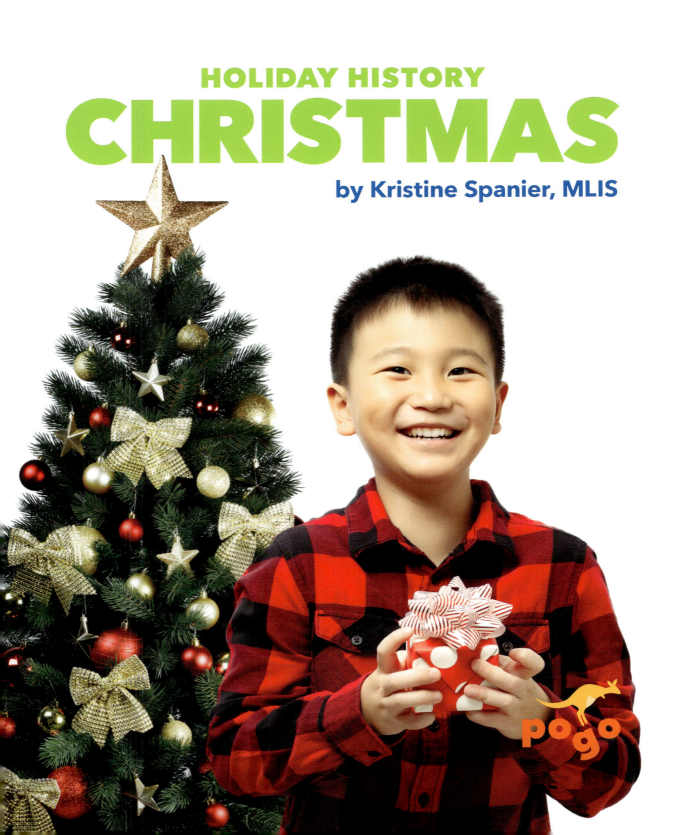

HOLIDAY HISTORY
CHRISTMAS

by Kristine Spanier, MLIS

Ideas for Parents and Teachers

Pogo Books let children practice reading informational text while introducing them to nonfiction features such as headings, labels, sidebars, maps, and diagrams, as well as a table of contents, glossary, and index.

Carefully leveled text with a strong photo match offers early fluent readers the support they need to succeed.

Before Reading

- "Walk" through the book and point out the various nonfiction features. Ask the student what purpose each feature serves.
- Look at the glossary together. Read and discuss the words.

Read the Book

- Have the child read the book independently.
- Invite him or her to list questions that arise from reading.

After Reading

- Discuss the child's questions. Talk about how he or she might find answers to those questions.
- Prompt the child to think more. Ask: Christmas traditions are discussed in this book. What other Christmas traditions do you know about?

Pogo Books are published by Jump!
5357 Penn Avenue South
Minneapolis, MN 55419
www.jumplibrary.com

Copyright © 2023 Jump!
International copyright reserved in all countries. No part of this book may be reproduced in any form without written permission from the publisher.

Library of Congress Cataloging-in-Publication Data

Names: Spanier, Kristine, author.
Title: Christmas / by Kristine Spanier, MLIS.
Description: Minneapolis, MN: Jump!, Inc., 2023.
Series: Holiday history | Includes index.
Audience: Ages 7-10
Identifiers: LCCN 2022014675 (print)
LCCN 2022014676 (ebook)
ISBN 9798885241199 (hardcover)
ISBN 9798885241205 (paperback)
ISBN 9798885241212 (ebook)
Subjects: LCSH: Christmas—Juvenile literature.
Classification: LCC GT4985.5 .S63 2023 (print)
LCC GT4985.5 (ebook)
DDC 394.2663—dc23/eng/20220408
LC record available at https://lccn.loc.gov/2022014675
LC ebook record available at https://lccn.loc.gov/2022014676

Editor: Eliza Leahy
Designer: Molly Ballanger

Photo Credits: Timmary/Shutterstock, cover (presents); Platslee/Shutterstock, cover (nativity); Yellowj/Shutterstock, 1 (tree); everydayplus/Shutterstock, 1 (boy); jamakosy/Shutterstock, 3; Dasha Petrenko/Shutterstock, 4; 1000 Words/Shutterstock, 5; JEAN-FRANCOIS MONIER/AFP/Getty, 6-7; Lea Rae/Shutterstock, 8; RTRO/Alamy, 9; Elizabethsalleebauer/Getty, 10-11; Llpeizer/Dreamstime, 11; Hero Images Inc./Alamy, 12-13; Shutterstock, 14-15 (background); The Picture Art Collection/Alamy, 14-15 (photo); bonchan/Shutterstock, 16; Fly View Productions/iStock, 17; Mikhail Markovskiy/Shutterstock, 18-19; SolStock/iStock, 20-21; Pixel-Shot/Shutterstock, 23.

Printed in the United States of America at Corporate Graphics in North Mankato, Minnesota.

TABLE OF CONTENTS

CHAPTER 1
The Birth of Jesus 4

CHAPTER 2
Christmas Traditions 8

CHAPTER 3
Christmas Around the World 16

QUICK FACTS & TOOLS
Christmas Place of Origin 22
Quick Facts 22
Glossary 23
Index 24
To Learn More 24

CHAPTER 1

THE BIRTH OF JESUS

More than 2,000 years ago, people all over Europe celebrated the **winter solstice**. They gathered around fires. They sang songs. They ate special meals.

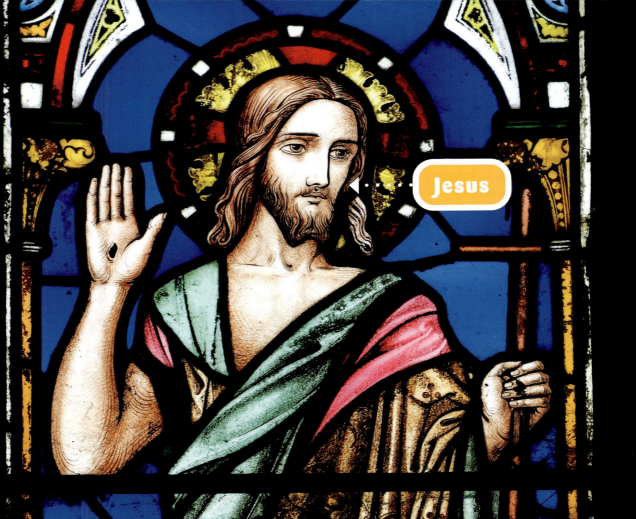

Jesus

Jesus was born around 6 BCE. He was a **religious** leader. In the 300s, **Christians** in the Roman **Empire** wanted to honor his birthday. But they didn't know when it was.

CHAPTER 1   5

They began celebrating it around the same time as the winter solstice. They chose December 25 as the date. The holiday came to be known as Christmas.

Many Christians go to church the night before on Christmas Eve. They sing. They light candles. Children act out the **Nativity**. These are called pageants.

> **DID YOU KNOW?**
>
> The **Bible** tells the story of Jesus's birth. He was laid in a **manger**. Animals were nearby. **Magi** brought gifts to baby Jesus.

CHAPTER 1

Nativity scene

CHAPTER 1

CHAPTER 2

CHRISTMAS TRADITIONS

Over time, more Christmas **traditions** started. Saint Nicholas once lived in what is now Türkiye. **Legend** says he gave gifts to children. He may have even put them in stockings! People brought this story to the Netherlands. Here, Saint Nicholas is called Sinterklaas.

Sinterklaas

In the United States, the name changed to Santa Claus. He is sometimes called Saint Nick. *The Night Before Christmas* is a poem. It was published in 1823. It describes Saint Nick traveling in a flying sleigh. It is pulled by eight reindeer. He visits homes. He puts gifts into stockings that hang by fireplaces.

CHAPTER 2

People still leave their stockings out for Santa. Some children leave cookies and milk out for him. Some leave carrots for his reindeer. Why? They might be hungry!

WHAT DO YOU THINK?

Not everyone celebrates Christmas. But it became a **national holiday** in the United States in 1870. Do you think it should be one? Why or why not?

stocking

CHAPTER 2 11

In 1843, Charles Dickens wrote the book *A Christmas Carol*. It is about a greedy man named Scrooge. He realizes he should be nicer and becomes **generous**. The story reminds people to help others during the Christmas season. Some organize food and gift drives. Others serve meals at shelters.

CHAPTER 2

CHAPTER 2

In 1848, Queen Victoria of England and her family gathered around a tree. It was decorated. Gifts hung from the branches. A picture was in a London newspaper.

After people saw it, they wanted their own Christmas trees! Today, many people get trees for their homes. They decorate them with ornaments and lights.

Queen Victoria

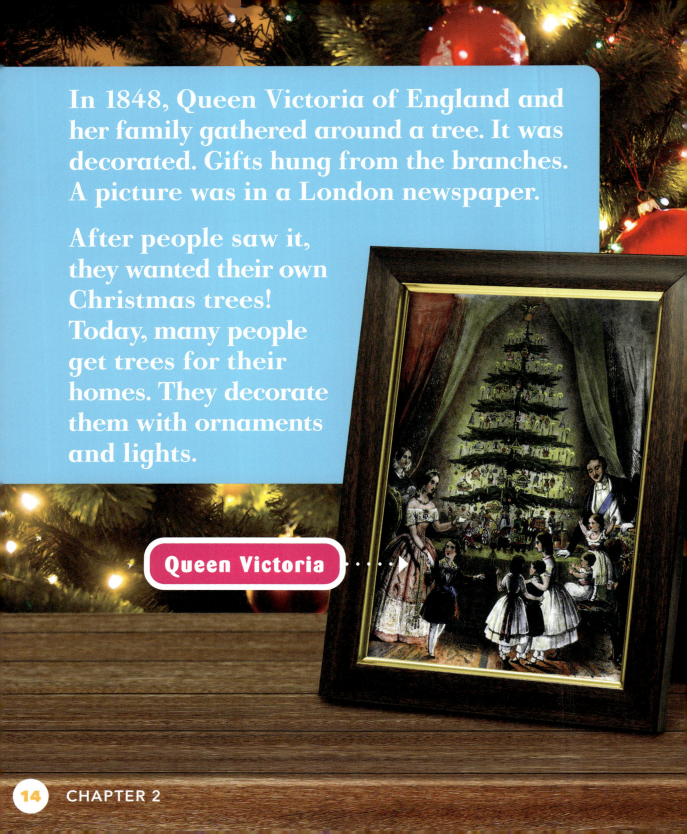

CHAPTER 2

TAKE A LOOK!

The colors red and green are often seen around Christmas. What are some other **symbols** of Christmas? Take a look!

CHAPTER 2   15

CHAPTER 3
CHRISTMAS AROUND THE WORLD

Christmas traditions differ around the world. In Japan, businesses stay open on December 25. People eat fried chicken. They enjoy strawberry cake for dessert.

Japanese Christmas cake

In Australia, it is summer in December. People go to the beach on Christmas Day.

CHAPTER 3   17

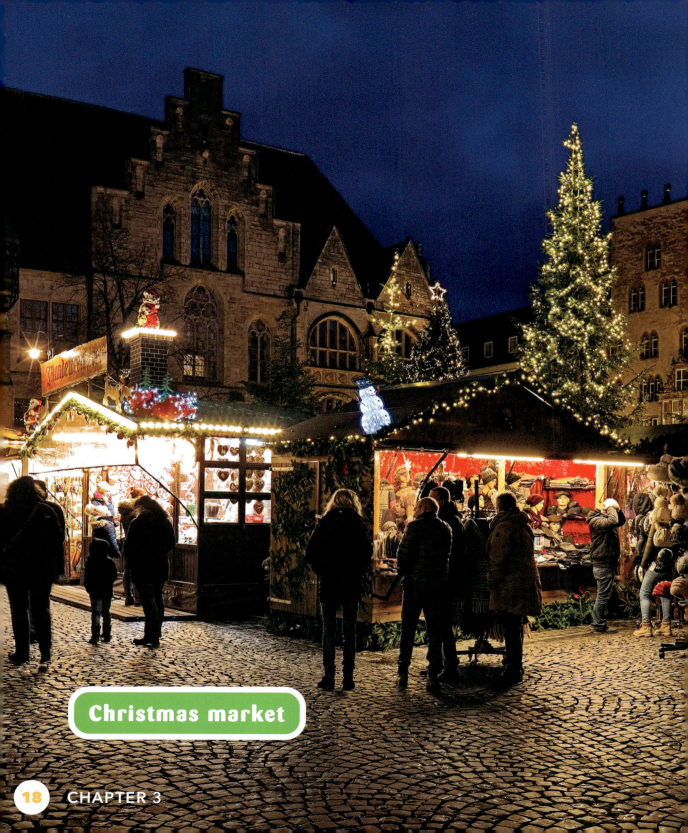
Christmas market

CHAPTER 3

Christmas markets fill town squares in Germany. People shop. They buy holiday foods and gifts. Gingerbread is a special treat!

DID YOU KNOW?

People celebrate Christmas for four months in the Philippines! The season starts in September. People go to parades, concerts, and parties.

CHAPTER 3 19

Christmas is a time for families to gather. They decorate their homes. They eat big meals together. They sing **carols**. Some go to church. Everyone is excited to open gifts!

WHAT DO YOU THINK?

People in different parts of the world have different Christmas traditions. Why do you think this is?

CHAPTER 3 21

QUICK FACTS & TOOLS

CHRISTMAS PLACE OF ORIGIN

QUICK FACTS

Date: December 25

Year of Origin: Early 300s

Place of Origin: Roman Empire

Common Symbols: Santa Claus, Nativity scenes, stars, angels, gifts, reindeer, Christmas trees, ornaments, lights

Foods: roasted ham or turkey, potatoes, cookies, pies, fruitcake

Traditions: worship services, gift giving, parades, decorating, pageants, caroling, baking, family meals

GLOSSARY

Bible: The sacred book of the Christian religion.

carols: Joyful songs about Christmas.

Christians: People who follow the religion based on the teachings of Jesus.

empire: A group of countries or states that has the same ruler.

generous: Willing and happy to give to and share with others.

legend: A story handed down from earlier generations that is often based on fact but is not entirely true.

Magi: The Wise Men who visited baby Jesus and brought him gifts.

manger: A large, open box that holds food for cattle or horses.

national holiday: A legal holiday established by the central government of a nation.

Nativity: A display or scene that shows the story and place of the birth of Jesus.

religious: Of or about the belief in, devotion to, and worship of a god.

symbols: Objects or designs that stand for, suggest, or represent something else.

traditions: Customs, ideas, or beliefs that are handed down from one generation to the next.

winter solstice: The event that marks the beginning of winter in the northern hemisphere.

QUICK FACTS & TOOLS

INDEX

Australia 17
Bible 6
Christians 5, 6
Christmas Eve 6
Christmas trees 14, 15
church 6, 20
cookies 11
Europe 4
Germany 19
gifts 6, 8, 9, 12, 14, 15, 19, 20
Japan 16
Jesus 5, 6
meals 4, 12, 20

Netherlands 8
pageants 6
Philippines 19
Queen Victoria 14
Roman Empire 5
Saint Nicholas 8, 9
sang 4, 6, 20
Santa Claus 9, 11, 15
stockings 8, 9, 11, 15
symbols 15
Türkiye 8
United States 9, 11
winter solstice 4, 6

TO LEARN MORE

Finding more information is as easy as 1, 2, 3.

1. Go to www.factsurfer.com
2. Enter "Christmas" into the search box.
3. Choose your book to see a list of websites.

24 QUICK FACTS & TOOLS